100 Dates.

100 handpicked date ideas for endless moments
of romance and adventure.

stella & soul
DESIGNS

Welcome to '100 Dates'.

In the pages that follow, you'll find a treasure trove
of date ideas carefully crafted to fit any budget,
ensuring that love, adventure, and connection
are accessible to all.

In every relationship, whether you've been together for years
or are just starting, it's essential to keep things fresh and exciting.
That's where our curated collection comes in.
By trying out these innovative date ideas, you'll breathe new life
into your connections, building lasting memories
that transcend the routine of daily life.

Imagine the joy of rediscovering each other in the glow of
a candlelit dinner, the thrill of an adventure in the great outdoors,
or the shared laughter at a local event. These experiences are
not only budget-friendly but also flexible, adapting to
the dynamics of your relationships.

So, whether you're seeking to reignite the spark in your
romantic partnership or deepen the bonds with your friends
and loved ones, you're in the right place.
Join us on a journey of love, laughter, and lasting memories
as we explore '100 Dates' together.

Let's make every moment unforgettable!

1
♥

Write a letter to each other.

Take a moment to write a few lines.
Here are some ideas: You can write down what you like most in the other person, what your favorite memory together is, what you wish to experience together in the future, ...
Then read the letters to each other.

How did you like the date?   Would you do it again?

Your favorite moment from this date?

2

At home Spa Day.

Treat yourselves with a relaxing Spa Day at home.
Get some face masks, eye patches (how about cucumber slices?), body peeling, bath salts etc.
Then light a few candles and play some slow music for your relaxing Spa Date at home.

How did you like the date?   Would you do it again?

Your favorite moment from this date?

3

Watch the sunset or sunrise.

Watching the sunset or sunrise always has a magical touch. Doing it together with your loved one makes it even more special. Just let yourselves be enchanted by this very special atmosphere during a sunset or sunrise.

How did you like the date?   Would you do it again?

☆ ☆ ☆ ☆ ☆   ☆ ☆ ☆ ☆ ☆

Your favorite moment from this date?

_____

_____

_____

4
♥

Share your happiest memory.

Get to know each other even better by sharing
your happiest memory each.
Depending on your mood, you can also share
the saddest memory, too.

How did you like the date?   Would you do it again?

☆☆☆☆☆   ☆☆☆☆☆

Your favorite moment from this date?

_____
_____
_____

5

Draw each other.

This date night where you draw each other will be lots of fun and very intimate at the same time. Get creative with the drawing style and which body part of each other you want to draw.

How did you like the date?

Would you do it again?

Your favorite moment from this date?

6

--- ♥ ---

Share your favorite book(s).

Tell each other about your favorite book(s) and why and how it has impacted you while reading it.
It can be any sort of book: fantasy, children's book, autobiography, mystery, romance, ...

How did you like the date? ☆☆☆☆☆

Would you do it again? ☆☆☆☆☆

Your favorite moment from this date?

7

Buy a small gift for each other.

Surprise each other with a small but thoughtful gift.
Set the maximum price beforehand (i.e. $5) and then choose something funny, cute, romantic, tasty, ...

How did you like the date? ☆☆☆☆☆

Would you do it again? ☆☆☆☆☆

Your favorite moment from this date?

8

Go low-tech.

Spend the evening without any technology:
no smartphones, candles instead of lights, books or
board games instead of TV, ...

How did you like the date?   Would you do it again?

⭐⭐⭐⭐⭐   ⭐⭐⭐⭐⭐

Your favorite moment from this date?

9

Discover your love languages.

We all give and receive love in 5 different ways: words of affirmation, acts of service, receiving gifts, quality time and physical touch.
Take an online quiz to discover your own love languages and discuss your results afterwards.

How did you like the date?

⭐ ⭐ ⭐ ⭐ ⭐

Would you do it again?

⭐ ⭐ ⭐ ⭐ ⭐

Your favorite moment from this date?

10

Massage each other.

Take some time to massage each other and
get closer on a physical level.
A couple's massage is a great way to experience intimacy in a
new way and increase feelings of affection.

How did you like the date?   Would you do it again?

☆☆☆☆☆   ☆☆☆☆☆

Your favorite moment from this date?

_____
_____
_____

11

Share your 5 favorite photos of each other.

We often see ourselves differently than others do
so by sharing your 5 favorite photos of the other person
you will understand deeper what your significant other loves
most about you.

How did you like the date?	Would you do it again?

Your favorite moment from this date?

12

Play (naked) Twister.

This is a very simple but super fun date idea so you don't need much more than the game itself, your partner and maybe some drinks & snacks.

How did you like the date?   Would you do it again?

☆☆☆☆☆   ☆☆☆☆☆

Your favorite moment from this date?

13

Recreate your first date.

Take a trip down memory lane by recreating the very first date you had and try to i.e. go back to the restaurant you had dinner. Alternatively, get creative at home at recreating your first date.

How did you like the date?

Would you do it again?

Your favorite moment from this date?

14

Share 3 things you love about yourself.

Sharing what you love most about yourself will deepen your relationship with your partner and help nurture your mutual admiration.

How did you like the date? ☆☆☆☆☆

Would you do it again? ☆☆☆☆☆

Your favorite moment from this date?

_____
_____
_____

15

Play hide & seek.

Enjoy this all-time favorite game from childhood memory and create a memorable, playful moment together.

How did you like the date?

Would you do it again?

Your favorite moment from this date?

16

Capture a day with a disposable camera.

Document one full day with a disposable camera and capture the simple joys and genuine emotions of that day on film - but remember: only one picture allowed per moment.

How did you like the date?   Would you do it again?

☆☆☆☆☆   ☆☆☆☆☆

Your favorite moment from this date?

17

Take a personality test together.

Kickstart a fascinating conversation by taking a personality test together, gaining new insights into each other's quirks and qualities.

How did you like the date? Would you do it again?

★ ★ ★ ★ ★   ★ ★ ★ ★ ★

Your favorite moment from this date?

_____
_____
_____

18

Spend a whole day cuddling on the couch.

Spend a cozy day on the couch, wrapped up in each other's arms,
and enjoy the simple pleasure of uninterrupted cuddling
with benefits from reducing stress to strengthening
your emotional bond.

How did you like the date? Would you do it again?

☆☆☆☆☆   ☆☆☆☆☆

Your favorite moment from this date?

_____

_____

_____

19

Ask each other 5 deep questions.

Enhance your emotional intimacy and strengthen your connection by asking each other 5 deep questions. This heartfelt dialogue will not only deepen your understanding of each other but also create a safe space for vulnerability.

Here are some examples:
What are your core values? What is your biggest dream?
What are your greatest fears? How do you envision our future together?
How do you define success in life? What are the key elements that you believe make our relationship special?

How did you like the date?   Would you do it again?

Your favorite moment from this date?

20

Create a couple bucket list.

Create your bucket list together filled with dreams and adventures you both wish to experience, solidifying your shared goals and aspirations.

How did you like the date?

Would you do it again?

Your favorite moment from this date?

21
♪

Go to the planetarium.

Step into the cosmos together as you visit the planetarium and let yourselves be mesmerized by the wonders of the universe and learn new facts about our stars and planets.

How did you like the date? Would you do it again?

☆☆☆☆☆ ☆☆☆☆☆

Your favorite moment from this date?

22

♫

Go to a drive-in cinema.

Enjoy the magic of old-school movie nights by heading to a drive-in cinema, where you can cuddle up in the comfort of your car and enjoy a classic movie under the open sky.

How did you like the date?   Would you do it again?

☆☆☆☆☆   ☆☆☆☆☆

Your favorite moment from this date?

23

♪

Go to a concert.

Enjoy a night out at a concert together, where you can listen to live music and the performance of your favorite band, dance and have fun, and create lasting memories.

How did you like the date?

Would you do it again?

Your favorite moment from this date?

24

Have a double date with friends.

Plan a fun double date with some friends or another couple, where you can all hang out together and have a good time as a group while i.e. cooking dinner or playing games.

How did you like the date?   Would you do it again?

☆☆☆☆☆   ☆☆☆☆☆

Your favorite moment from this date?

25
♪

Learn a new language together.

Create a deeper connection side by side as you both take on the adventure of learning a new language together, sharing the challenges and triumphs along the way.

How did you like the date?   Would you do it again?

Your favorite moment from this date?

26

♪

Go to a burlesque or drag show.

Experience an evening of vibrant entertainment and self-expression by attending a fun burlesque or drag show together, where you'll be dazzled by the stunning performances and celebrate individuality in style.

How did you like the date?

☆☆☆☆☆

Would you do it again?

☆☆☆☆☆

Your favorite moment from this date?

27

♫

Create a Spotify playlist and dance to it.

Create your very own couple Spotify playlist together
and let the music move you as you dance to your
favorite tunes, creating your very own soundtrack
in your private little dance party.

How did you like the date?   Would you do it again?

☆ ☆ ☆ ☆ ☆   ☆ ☆ ☆ ☆ ☆

Your favorite moment from this date?

28

♪

Visit a museum or art gallery.

Explore the world of art and culture together and visit a museum or art gallery, where you can admire masterpieces, share interpretations, and appreciate the beauty of human creativity side by side.

How did you like the date?　　　Would you do it again?

☆☆☆☆☆　　　　　　　☆☆☆☆☆

Your favorite moment from this date?

_____
_____
_____

29

Go bowling.

Strike up some fun and friendly competition and go bowling together. Enjoy a night full of laughs, strikes, and spares, making lasting memories while knocking down pins.

How did you like the date? Would you do it again?

☆☆☆☆☆ ☆☆☆☆☆

Your favorite moment from this date?

_____

_____

_____

30

♪

Visit an abandoned place.

Go on an adventure to explore an abandoned place together, uncovering forgotten stories and secrets, and sharing a thrilling and mysterious journey together.

How did you like the date?   Would you do it again?

☆☆☆☆☆   ☆☆☆☆☆

Your favorite moment from this date?

31
♪

Throw a casino night.

Transform your home into a mini casino and
host a lively casino night together, trying your luck
with various games, and relishing the excitement
of a glamorous evening without leaving your doorstep.

How did you like the date?   Would you do it again?

Your favorite moment from this date?

32

♪

Go to a festival.

Dive into the world of music and attend a music festival
together, dancing to the beats, sharing the excitement,
and creating unforgettable moments
in this unique atmosphere.

How did you like the date?   Would you do it again?

☆☆☆☆☆   ☆☆☆☆☆

Your favorite moment from this date?

33

♪

Go to a karaoke bar.

Unleash your inner rock stars as you head to a karaoke bar and take the stage, can sing your hearts out, share laughter, and create a memorable night filled with music and fun.

How did you like the date?   Would you do it again?

☆ ☆ ☆ ☆ ☆   ☆ ☆ ☆ ☆ ☆

Your favorite moment from this date?

_____
_____
_____

34

♪

Volunteer together.

Give back to your community and strengthen your bond by volunteering together. Working hand in hand to make a positive impact through acts of kindness and compassion will create meaningful memories.

How did you like the date?   Would you do it again?

★★★★★   ★★★★★

Your favorite moment from this date?

35

Play "never have I ever".

Spice up your evening with a game of 'Never Have I Ever'.
Take turns sharing unique experiences and secrets
that might reveal new sides of yourselves.

How did you like the date?   Would you do it again?

Your favorite moment from this date?

36

Draw each other.

Discover your artistic sides and bond on a creative level by drawing each other. You might be surprised how you capture one another's unique personalities and features.

How did you like the date?

☆☆☆☆☆

Would you do it again?

☆☆☆☆☆

Your favorite moment from this date?

_____
_____
_____

37
♪

Throw a "Harry Potter" Night.

Step into the world of wizards and magic as you host a 'Harry Potter' night, complete with themed decorations, movie marathons, and magical treats, creating a whimsical and spellbinding experience together.

How did you like the date?   Would you do it again?

Your favorite moment from this date?

38

♫

Go to a stand-up comedy show.

Laugh your hearts out together by attending
a stand-up comedy show and enjoy a night of humor,
witty performances that will leave you with
memorable inside jokes.

How did you like the date? Would you do it again?

☆ ☆ ☆ ☆ ☆   ☆ ☆ ☆ ☆ ☆

Your favorite moment from this date?

39

Go to an amusement park.

Rekindle your inner child and enjoy an exciting day together at an amusement park. Embrace the thrill of roller coasters, indulge in unlimited cotton candy and create unforgettable moments filled with excitement and laughter.

How did you like the date?

Would you do it again?

Your favorite moment from this date?

40

♫

Go strawberry or fruit picking.

Escape to the countryside and enjoy a day of wholesome fun
by picking fresh strawberries or fruits together.
Fill your baskets with ripe, sun-kissed treasures and
enjoy the simple pleasure of harvesting
your own delicious bounty.

How did you like the date?   Would you do it again?

☆☆☆☆☆   ☆☆☆☆☆

Your favorite moment from this date?

41

Candle light dinner at home.

Set the scene for a romantic evening and enjoy a candlelit dinner at home with soft, flickering candlelight and a delicious meal. Create an intimate atmosphere at home that enhances your connection and sparks meaningful conversation.

How did you like the date?	Would you do it again?

Your favorite moment from this date?

42

--- 🍴 ---

Have a picknick in a park.

Embrace the beauty of the outdoors by having a picnic in a nearby park. Spread out a blanket, enjoy some snacks, and create a relaxing and memorable day together.

How did you like the date?   Would you do it again?

☆☆☆☆☆   ☆☆☆☆☆

Your favorite moment from this date?

_____
_____
_____

43

Bake a cake together.

Create some sweet memories as you team up to create a delicious cake together. From mixing ingredients to decorating the final masterpiece, you'll bond over the joy of creating something sweet and memorable.

How did you like the date?

Would you do it again?

Your favorite moment from this date?

44

Order for the other person.

Go to a restaurant and add a touch of surprise to your dining experience by taking turns ordering for each other - let's see how well you know each others culinary preferences.

How did you like the date?

⭐ ⭐ ⭐ ⭐ ⭐

Would you do it again?

⭐ ⭐ ⭐ ⭐ ⭐

Your favorite moment from this date?

45

Test 3 fancy coffee shops.

Turn your coffee cravings into a fun adventure as you test three fancy coffee shops. Sip on unique brews, indulge in decadent pastries, and rate your top picks, all while sharing laughs and caffeinated moments.

How did you like the date?

Would you do it again?

Your favorite moment from this date?

46

Have breakfast at a farmer's market.

Start your day with a fresh and flavorful twist by enjoying breakfast at a bustling farmer's market. Savor local produce, artisanal treats, and the vibrant atmosphere, creating a wholesome and delicious morning together.

How did you like the date?

☆☆☆☆☆

Would you do it again?

☆☆☆☆☆

Your favorite moment from this date?

_____
_____
_____

47

Make your own Sushi.

Roll up your sleeves and dive into a sushi-making extravaganza! Get creative with colorful ingredients, experiment with unique combinations, and have a blast crafting your very own sushi masterpieces together.

How did you like the date?

Would you do it again?

Your favorite moment from this date?

48

Join a wine & cheese tasting.

Indulge in the finer things in life with a wine and cheese tasting.
Sample a variety of wines and cheeses, share your thoughts
on flavors, and enjoy a sophisticated yet fun
culinary experience together.

How did you like the date?	Would you do it again?

☆☆☆☆☆	☆☆☆☆☆

Your favorite moment from this date?

49

Go on a pub crawl.

Get ready for a wild night out as you go on a pub crawl together!
Explore the best local watering holes, sample their quirkiest
drinks, and challenge each other to hilarious pub games,
all while sharing laughs and memorable moments.

How did you like the date?   Would you do it again?

Your favorite moment from this date?

50

--- 🍴 ---

Throw a pin and choose the closest restaurant.

Spice up your dining adventure with a playful twist!
Throw a pin on a map and dine at the closest restaurant
it lands on. Whether it's a hidden gem or a quirky spot,
you're in for a spontaneous culinary journey filled with surprises
and plenty of laughs!

How did you like the date?   Would you do it again?

☆ ☆ ☆ ☆ ☆   ☆ ☆ ☆ ☆ ☆

Your favorite moment from this date?

_____
_____
_____

51

Make your own pizza.

Get ready for a pizza-making party that's not only delicious but also loads of fun! Roll out the dough, pile on your favorite toppings, and have a blast challenging each other to create the most outrageous and tasty homemade pizzas ever.

How did you like the date?

Would you do it again?

Your favorite moment from this date?

52

🍴

Go on a Food Crawl.

Prepare your taste buds for a gastronomic marathon with a food crawl extravaganza! For starters, main course and dessert, hop between three different restaurants. Indulge in a variety of dishes, and rate your favorite bites in a thrilling foodie competition.

How did you like the date?
☆☆☆☆☆

Would you do it again?
☆☆☆☆☆

Your favorite moment from this date?

_____
_____
_____

53

Make your own ice cream.

Transform your kitchen into an ice cream wonderland as you both craft your own delicious ice cream flavors. Experiment with exciting combinations, load up on toppings, and savor the joy of making and enjoying your personalized frozen treats together.

How did you like the date?

Would you do it again?

Your favorite moment from this date?

54

Dine in the dark.

Try something unique by dining in complete darkness. Share an intriguing and sensory adventure as you rely on your senses other than sight, heightening your taste, touch, and conversation for a truly unforgettable meal.

How did you like the date?

☆☆☆☆☆

Would you do it again?

☆☆☆☆☆

Your favorite moment from this date?

55

Have dessert for breakfast.

Switch up your morning routine with a delightful twist — have dessert for breakfast! Indulge in sweet treats, pastries, or your favorite desserts to kickstart your day with a dash of sweetness and fun.

How did you like the date?

Would you do it again?

Your favorite moment from this date?

56

Host an at home cooking competition.

Add some excitement to your night by hosting an at-home cooking competition. Take turns preparing dishes and see who can come up with the most delicious meal.
It's a fun way to bond and enjoy some great food together.

How did you like the date?   Would you do it again?

Your favorite moment from this date?

57

Invent a new recipe.

Get your creative culinary hats on and invent a
brand-new recipe together! Experiment with ingredients,
flavors, and techniques as you collaborate to create a unique dish
that reflects your taste and culinary ingenuity.

How did you like the date?   Would you do it again?

☆ ☆ ☆ ☆ ☆   ☆ ☆ ☆ ☆ ☆

Your favorite moment from this date?

58

Have a fondue night.

Turn your evening into a fondue adventure! Gather around a bubbling pot of cheese or chocolate, dip in an assortment of delicious treats, and enjoy a cozy and interactive night of dipping and savoring.

How did you like the date?
☆☆☆☆☆

Would you do it again?
☆☆☆☆☆

Your favorite moment from this date?

59

Cook a 3 course dinner using only pantry ingredients.

Challenge your culinary skills by cooking a three-course dinner using only pantry ingredients. Get creative with what's on hand and revel in the satisfaction of a delicious and resourceful meal.

How did you like the date? Would you do it again?

Your favorite moment from this date?

60

Host a test taste (blindfolded).

Turn your dining experience into an exciting taste test challenge! Blindfold each other, sample different dishes, and see who can guess the ingredients and flavors correctly.

How did you like the date? Would you do it again?

☆☆☆☆☆ ☆☆☆☆☆

Your favorite moment from this date?

_____
_____
_____

61

Feed the ducks.

Enjoy a charming day at the park by feeding the ducks together.
Grab some duck-friendly food, head to a nearby pond,
and relish the simple joy of watching these feathered friends
gather around for a snack.

How did you like the date?   Would you do it again?

Your favorite moment from this date?

62

Go camping.

Escape the hustle and bustle of everyday life and embrace the great outdoors by going camping together. Set up a cozy campsite, cook over an open fire, and create lasting memories under the starry night sky.

How did you like the date?

Would you do it again?

Your favorite moment from this date?

63

Go to a flea market.

Explore hidden treasures and unique finds as you spend the day at a flea market together. Wander through rows of vintage items, quirky crafts, sharing laughs and discovering one-of-a-kind gems.

How did you like the date? Would you do it again?

☆ ☆ ☆ ☆ ☆ ☆ ☆ ☆ ☆ ☆

Your favorite moment from this date?

64

Be a tourist in your own city.

Take a break from the everyday routine and enjoy a day of exploration by being a tourist in your own city.
Visit iconic landmarks, try out local attractions, and rediscover the charm of your hometown together.

How did you like the date?   Would you do it again?

☆☆☆☆☆   ☆☆☆☆☆

Your favorite moment from this date?

65

Cowork together.

Combine work and quality time by coworking together. Whether at home or a cozy cafe, share a workspace and boost each other's productivity while enjoying each other's company throughout the day.

How did you like the date?   Would you do it again?

Your favorite moment from this date?

66

Go dancing.

Put on your dancing shoes and hit the dance floor together!
Enjoy the rhythm, movement, and the sheer joy of dancing
as you let loose and create unforgettable memories
on the dance floor.

How did you like the date? ★★★★★

Would you do it again? ★★★★★

Your favorite moment from this date?

67

Have a YES day.

Declare a YES day and embark on a spontaneous adventure where you say 'yes' to every opportunity or idea that comes your way. From trying new foods to exploring new places, it's a day of limitless fun and excitement together.

How did you like the date?   Would you do it again?

Your favorite moment from this date?

68

Visit a favorite spot from your childhood.

Take a nostalgic trip down memory lane by visiting a beloved spot from your childhood. Share stories, reminisce about your past adventures, and create new memories together as you revisit a special place from your youth.

How did you like the date?   Would you do it again?

☆☆☆☆☆   ☆☆☆☆☆

Your favorite moment from this date?

69

Visit a dog park or cat café.

Indulge in your love for animals by spending time at a dog park or visiting a cat café. Whether it's playing with furry friends at the park or sipping coffee surrounded by adorable cats, it's a heartwarming and joyful experience together.

How did you like the date?

☆ ☆ ☆ ☆ ☆

Would you do it again?

☆ ☆ ☆ ☆ ☆

Your favorite moment from this date?

_____
_____
_____
_____

70

Wander a new neighborhood.

Enjoy an urban adventure as you venture through an unfamiliar neighborhood hand in hand. Stroll the streets, discover quaint shops and cafes, and savor the excitement of uncovering new places and experiences together.

How did you like the date? Would you do it again?

☆☆☆☆☆ ☆☆☆☆☆

Your favorite moment from this date?

_____
_____
_____

71

Go shopping and choose clothes for each other.

Turn shopping into a playful fashion challenge by choosing clothes for each other. Explore the stores, pick out stylish outfits, and share some laughs as you discover each other's fashion tastes and preferences.

How did you like the date?

Would you do it again?

Your favorite moment from this date?

72

Google a free activity in your area and do it.

Spontaneously embrace local adventure by googling a free activity in your area and giving it a go together.
It's a fun way to explore your surroundings, discover hidden gems, and enjoy an unexpected and cost-free experience.

How did you like the date? Would you do it again?

☆☆☆☆☆ ☆☆☆☆☆

Your favorite moment from this date?

73

Create a scavenger hunt.

Put your creativity to the test and design a personalized scavenger hunt for each other. Craft clues that lead to meaningful places or memories, and embark on an adventure of discovery and surprise, strengthening your bond along the way.

How did you like the date?

Would you do it again?

Your favorite moment from this date?

74

Go on an alphabet date with your first names.

Create a fun and personalized date by taking an 'alphabet date' challenge using the first letters of your names.
Pick activities, places, or foods that correspond to each letter of your names and enjoy a day filled with surprises and shared experiences.

How did you like the date?   Would you do it again?

☆☆☆☆☆   ☆☆☆☆☆

Your favorite moment from this date?

_____
_____
_____

75

Swap houses with a friend for a weekend.

Add excitement to your weekend by swapping houses
with a friend for a unique change of scenery.
Experience life in a new neighborhood and create memories
in a different home-away-from-home.

How did you like the date?   Would you do it again?

★ ★ ★ ★ ★   ★ ★ ★ ★ ★

Your favorite moment from this date?

Drive / walk 30min in one direction.

Set out on a spontaneous journey by driving or walking for 30 minutes in one direction, and see where the path takes you. Whether you stumble upon a hidden gem or just enjoy the adventure, it's a simple and fun way to explore together.

How did you like the date?
☆☆☆☆☆

Would you do it again?
☆☆☆☆☆

Your favorite moment from this date?
_____
_____
_____

77

Go on a photography walk.

Try something new and go on a photography walk.
Each of you can snap three photos that capture moments or
scenes that resonate with you emotionally or remind you
of something special, creating a visual journey
of shared memories.

How did you like the date?   Would you do it again?

Your favorite moment from this date?

78

Sign up for dance lessons together.

Add some rhythm and romance to your relationship by signing up for dance lessons together. Whether it's salsa, tango, or any other dance style, you'll have a blast learning new moves and strengthening your connection on the dance floor.

How did you like the date? Would you do it again?

☆☆☆☆☆ ☆☆☆☆☆

Your favorite moment from this date?

_____

_____

_____

79

Visits the spots of a movie that was filmed in your area.

Go on a movie-inspired tour of your local area by visiting the iconic spots where a film was shot. Follow in the footsteps of your favorite movie characters, share laughs, and create your own cinematic memories as you explore the real-life settings of a beloved film.

How did you like the date?   Would you do it again?

Your favorite moment from this date?

80

Go to a park with a blanket and watch the clouds.

Embrace the serenity of nature as you head to a nearby park with a cozy blanket in tow. Lay back, watch the clouds drift by, and let your imaginations run wild as you share a tranquil and dreamy moment together.

How did you like the date?　　　Would you do it again?

☆☆☆☆☆　　　☆☆☆☆☆

Your favorite moment from this date?

_____
_____
_____

81

Go inline skating.

Get your adrenaline pumping and enjoy an active day together by going inline skating. Glide through parks or along scenic paths, holding hands, and sharing a thrilling and fun-filled adventure on wheels.

How did you like the date?

☆☆☆☆☆

Would you do it again?

☆☆☆☆☆

Your favorite moment from this date?

Play paddle tennis together.

Hit the court and engage in a lively game of paddle tennis together. Challenge each other to a friendly match, work on your teamwork, and enjoy the excitement of this active and dynamic sport.

How did you like the date?   Would you do it again?

☆☆☆☆☆   ☆☆☆☆☆

Your favorite moment from this date?

83

Go swimming at a lake.

Dive into the refreshing waters of a nearby lake and enjoy a day of swimming together. Whether you're splashing around or simply floating and relaxing, it's a perfect way to soak up the sun and create wonderful memories in the great outdoors.

How did you like the date?   Would you do it again?

Your favorite moment from this date?

84

Play mini golf.

Embrace some friendly competition by playing a round of mini golf together. Navigate the whimsical obstacles, share laughs, and see who can conquer the tricky course with style and skill.

How did you like the date?   Would you do it again?

☆☆☆☆☆   ☆☆☆☆☆

Your favorite moment from this date?

_____
_____
_____

85

Take a long walk together (no phones).

Unplug and connect on a deeper level by taking a long, leisurely walk together without the distractions of phones.
Stroll through your favorite paths or explore new ones,
share stories, and savor the simple joy of each other's company.

How did you like the date?   Would you do it again?

Your favorite moment from this date?

86

Play volleyball together.

Set up a beach or backyard volleyball match for a playful and active date. Dive for spectacular saves, cheer each other on, and create a memorable day filled with sunshine, sandy toes, and friendly competition.

How did you like the date?

☆☆☆☆☆

Would you do it again?

☆☆☆☆☆

Your favorite moment from this date?

87

Go pedal boating.

Set sail on a fun and leisurely pedal boating excursion together. Glide across the water, enjoy the scenery, and bask in each other's company as you pedal your way through a relaxing and enjoyable aquatic adventure.

How did you like the date?   Would you do it again?

☆☆☆☆☆   ☆☆☆☆☆

Your favorite moment from this date?

88

Hike the nearest mountain.

Turn your hike into a playful mountain adventure!
Climb the nearest peak together, explore hidden nooks and crannies, and see who can spot the most interesting wildlife or unique rock formations along the way.
It's a fun and exhilarating journey to the top!

How did you like the date? Would you do it again?

☆☆☆☆☆   ☆☆☆☆☆

Your favorite moment from this date?

89

Watch a sports game.

Get ready for some excitement by watching a sports game together. Cheer for your favorite team, enjoy the thrill of the match, and revel in the camaraderie and energy of the crowd while creating unforgettable memories.

How did you like the date?   Would you do it again?

Your favorite moment from this date?

90

Go skydiving.

Take your love for adventure to new heights by going skydiving together. Feel the rush of wind, enjoy breathtaking views, and share an unforgettable adrenaline-pumping experience that will bond you like never before.

How did you like the date?   Would you do it again?

☆☆☆☆☆   ☆☆☆☆☆

Your favorite moment from this date?

91

Play billiard together.

Hit the billiards table and engage in a friendly game of pool together. Showcase your skills, strategize your shots, and enjoy the casual competition while sharing some laughs and quality time.

How did you like the date?   Would you do it again?

Your favorite moment from this date?

92

Run or walk a charity 5k.

Combine fitness and philanthropy by participating in a charity 5k run or walk together. Join the cause, work towards a shared goal, and enjoy the uplifting atmosphere of a charity event while making a positive impact.

How did you like the date? Would you do it again?

☆☆☆☆☆ ☆☆☆☆☆

Your favorite moment from this date?

_____
_____
_____

93

Learn a TikTok dance together.

Get in on the TikTok trend and have a blast learning a popular dance together. Whether you master the moves or end up with some hilarious bloopers, it's a fun and lighthearted way to bond through music and movement.

How did you like the date?

Would you do it again?

Your favorite moment from this date?

94

Join a Yoga class together.

Find your inner zen and enhance your physical and mental well-being by joining a yoga class together. Stretch, breathe, and relax as you embark on a journey of mindfulness and self-care as a couple.

How did you like the date? Would you do it again?

☆☆☆☆☆   ☆☆☆☆☆

Your favorite moment from this date?

_____
_____
_____

95

Go for a bike ride.

Enjoy the great outdoors and the thrill of the ride by going for a bike adventure together. Explore scenic trails, pedal along picturesque routes, and share in the joy of an active and refreshing outing.

How did you like the date?   Would you do it again?

Your favorite moment from this date?

96

Go indoor climbing.

Take your adventure to new heights by going indoor climbing together. Challenge each other on the climbing walls, conquer obstacles, and celebrate your achievements in a thrilling and active date.

How did you like the date?   Would you do it again?

☆☆☆☆☆   ☆☆☆☆☆

Your favorite moment from this date?

97

Rent a kayak or canoue.

Turn your kayaking or canoeing adventure into a splashy,
fun-filled day! Engage in friendly water fights,
try synchronized paddling, and make a splash as you enjoy
a lively and memorable day together.

How did you like the date?   Would you do it again?

Your favorite moment from this date?

98

Play darts together.

Sharpen your aim and engage in a friendly game of darts together. Take turns aiming for the bullseye, share some laughs over near misses, and enjoy a laid-back yet exciting indoor activity.

How did you like the date?

☆☆☆☆☆

Would you do it again?

☆☆☆☆☆

Your favorite moment from this date?

___
___
___

99

Go to a minor league sports event.

Experience the thrill of sports by attending a minor league event together. Cheer for the local team, indulge in stadium snacks, and savor the atmosphere of a live sports event while creating lasting memories.

How did you like the date?

Would you do it again?

Your favorite moment from this date?

100

Complete a HIIT workout together.

Boost your fitness levels and share the burn by completing a high-intensity interval training (HIIT) workout together. Push each other through the exercises, break a sweat, and enjoy the sense of accomplishment as you conquer a challenging workout as a team.

How did you like the date?

Would you do it again?

Your favorite moment from this date?

Thank you

for embarking on this unforgettable journey
with us, and we hope these date ideas
have filled your life with joy, love,
and cherished memories.

stella & soul
DESIGNS

Stella & Soul is a small female business with passion for paper products and design
and we hope our thoughtfully created products bring you joy
and make your daily life a little more special.

Have you seen our One line a day and Manifestation Journal?

Printed in Great Britain
by Amazon